LET US GO NOW TO

Bethlehem

DAILY DEVOTIONS
FOR ADVENT AND CHRISTMAS

TODD OUTCALT

UPPER
ROOM BOOKS®
NASHVILLE

To Chelsey, Michael, and Logan
For Christmases past, present, and yet to come

———

Front cover images: iStock and Shutterstock
Back cover image: 123RF
Cover design: Bruce Gore | Gore Studio, Inc.
Interior design: PerfecType, Nashville, TN

Print ISBN: 978-0-8358-1930-5
Mobi ISBN: 978-0-8358-1931-2
Epub ISBN: 978-0-8358-1932-9

Printed in the United States of America

CONTENTS

Part 2: Christmas

O Little Town of Bethlehem

O little town of Bethlehem;
How still we see thee lie;
Above thy deep and dreamless sleep
The silent stars go by:
Yet in thy dark streets shineth
The everlasting Light;
The hopes and fears of all the years
Are met in thee tonight.

For Christ is born of Mary,
And gathered all above,
While mortals sleep, the angels keep
Their watch of wond'ring love.
O morning stars, together
Proclaim the holy birth!
And praises sing to God the King,
And peace to men on earth.

—Phillips Brooks (1835–1893)

INTRODUCTION

When the angels had left them and gone into heaven, the shepherds said to one another, "Let us go now to Bethlehem and see this thing that has taken place, which the Lord has made known to us."

—LUKE 2:15

We are all people of peculiar and particular histories. We have our stories to tell—our sagas of challenges overcome, dreams dashed and fulfilled, adventures enjoyed, failures and successes, the names and faces of heroes and heroines. If offered the opportunity, we probably could list the highlights of our lives, along with the various low points, on a linear timeline.

But the truth is, we do not experience life in a linear fashion. Yes, we have beginnings and endings, mountains and valleys. But our existence is always experienced in the uncertainties of the great adventures that are before us and the foundation and learning that we pull behind. We can only learn from the past, and we anticipate what might be in the future.

History and past lives, on the other hand, are quite different.

We have a tendency to chart the course of history from some high vantage point, where we make judgments about people and places and momentous outcomes from an omniscient point of view—even though our knowledge of these past experiences is, at best, marginal and our vision, looking back, fraught with uncertainties and the limitations of time. We rarely see life as an adventure, as a series of opportunities and challenges that call to the best of our character and faith. But in large part, I hope this small book of Advent and Christmas devotions will offer such an opportunity—a slight respite from the seasons of busyness and preparation and joy in which to pause, reflect, and perhaps enter the great adventure of faith as a journey to Bethlehem.

When we undertake any journey of faith, we do so by taking one step at a time. We never arrive at our destinations—especially spiritual ones—without struggle, persistence, and the help and assistance of others. Bethlehem is the call to come and see what God has done—and what God can do—in our lives. Bethlehem is the call to choose Jesus as our guide and our destination.

Our steps of faith may be taking us ever closer to some destination we set out toward many years before: perhaps a decision, a call, or some great work we wish to accomplish for God. Or our journey could be of the interior variety—a closer relationship with God, a deeper concern for others, or intentional conversations we need to have with those we love. We might undertake the journey of the season to find more hope or joy in an otherwise drab or mundane experience.

It is likely that most people reading this book have never been to the little town of Bethlehem. But that is of little consequence to the actual adventure of *journeying there*, to the adventure of discovery that awaits the mystery and wonder in the birth of Jesus. These devotions, I hope, can strengthen the faith of all readers who have ever pondered the meaning of Christ's birth or have ever desired to move into some new adventure of the heart and mind. I hope readers can discover something new they may have overlooked in "the old, old story" (UMH, no. 156).

I have been to Bethlehem a couple of times in my life. I have entered its walls, and I have touched the traditional stones commemorating the birthplace of Jesus in the Church of the Nativity. I have passed along the flame taken from the grotto of the Church of the Nativity in subsequent Advents and Christmases as the Peace Light of Christ has made its way around the world— a flame passed from person to person. And I have witnessed the hardships and suffering surrounding Bethlehem and the peace that eludes, even now, the people who populate this small village outside of Jerusalem.

And yet, the Bethlehem of the Bible—the one described from the vantage point of Gospel writers, shepherds, prophets, and poets—is not really a place we can reach by walking or completing a pilgrimage. We can arrive there only by faith, much like many of the saints longed for a celestial city—a place not made by human hands but eternal in the heavens. We are still journeying toward Jesus—although, he is, in fact, the very One who is guiding us, through the Holy Spirit. If we want to go to Bethlehem, if we long to journey there, we need not purchase an airline ticket. We can watch, listen, serve, and grow as we make our way to Jesus. And even if we are still curious or have questions about him, he awaits us at the end of the journey, just as the infant Jesus awaited the shepherds and the magi.

Jesus is the one we are seeking. It is the journey of a lifetime, a spiritual one, and it will last all life long. Perhaps this little devotional can help you along the way and offer new steps during the Advent and Christmas seasons. Hopefully, you can find yourself listening to these concise scripture promises, pondering a deep thought, or even whispering a prayer. You might discover new ways to serve others or begin again. Or you might undertake this journey with others—in a small group or as a family.

Are you willing to take the journey? Set out for Bethlehem. Let's see what Jesus has in store for us. We can go together.

So, let us be on our way.

Amen.

HOW TO USE THIS BOOK

This book is written for both personal and small-group use. There are devotions for each of the twenty-eight* days of Advent, for the twelve days of Christmas, and for the day of the Epiphany. All told, this book can be used as a devotional tool or a study guide for six weeks.

Readers can make this study a pilgrimage, of sorts, through the days of Advent and Christmas on their way to Bethlehem. And small groups or classes can use a week at a time (seven devotions) to accompany the study guide at the back of this book, a guide that contains questions for reflection and conversation. The guide may also be used by a leader to formulate additional ideas, or the scripture lessons of the week may be used to expand knowledge of the biblical text accompanied by these thoughts and questions.

As a suggestion for personal devotion, I would recommend placing this book in a location one can visit each day—a favorite chair, a porch, or a table beside the fireplace. As such, the devotions will not be forgotten but can become a daily part of one's routine—a discipline that one can return to every morning or evening.

Finally, the questions for individual reflection or group discussion in the back of the book can be used once a week for further study and review.

---

* The number of days of Advent varies from twenty-two to twenty-eight, depending upon the particular year.

ADVENT

AN ADVENT PRAYER

No longer shall we dream of the old year
As in these weeks, anticipation wraps
Hearth and home
And comes full circle in the time
Where joy inscribes the new maps
Of love
Which have come near.

Being Alert

"But about that day or hour no one knows, neither the angels in heaven, nor the Son, but only the Father. Beware, keep alert; for you do not know when the time will come. It is like a man going on a journey, when he leaves home and puts his slaves in charge, each with his work, and commands the doorkeeper to be on the watch. Therefore, keep awake—for you do not know when the master of the house will come, in the evening, or at midnight, or at cockcrow, or at dawn, or else he may find you asleep when he comes suddenly."

—MARK 13:32-36

Some years ago, during a lengthy trip through Europe via rail, my wife and I found ourselves perplexed by the myriad options available to us at the train station in Rome. There were dozens of names and numbers displayed on the overhead schedules, trains coming and going, and thousands of people clamoring about with their families and luggage. In short, we were bewildered, frightened, and certainly lost.

Fortunately, we had a guide who met us at the station and gave us both reassurance and instruction. "Here is what you watch for," she told us. "Don't become distracted by the hustle and bustle around you. Always keep an eye out for the porter. He will be on board and will give you instruction as to when you have arrived at your destination."

Our guide was most helpful. And I'm not sure we would have made it through Europe without her calm assurances and her steady hand.

Advent begins—and in fact, the entirety of the Christian journey begins—at the point where we accept Jesus as our Guide and begin to walk with his calm assurances in the midst of our fears. He's going to meet us, he tells us. He's going to show up, even if we don't know when or how. Jesus even invites us to look for his presence in the lives and faces of others. He may come to us at unexpected moments or when we are most tired or worn or confused. He may show up at the beginning or appear at the end of all things, when we least expect God's redemption or grace.

What a promise!

So, as Mark 13 tells us, we need to be ready for Jesus' coming at all times, including during our Advent journey. We may encounter Jesus in those closest to us: a spouse, a son or daughter, a grandparent, or a neighbor across the street. The way to Bethlehem is saturated with starts and stops, with both darkness and light, with angels and shepherds. We may discover that, like that of the shepherds (see Luke 2:8-20), our journey to Bethlehem is not far; or we may have to travel a great distance to get where we need to be, as did the magi (see Matthew 2:1-12).

But the journey, as with every journey, begins with a single step: a step of faith; a lively step of confidence and watchfulness. Where do you need to be with God? Where might God be guiding you? What are you waiting for?

Prayer: *Lord Emmanuel, let me be alert and watchful for your arrival, for your guidance. Help me not to fall asleep or be blinded by arrogance or pride. Help me to watch through the night as I anticipate the dawn. Strengthen me for the journey ahead. Amen.*

ADVENT
Day 2

Transformation

Present your bodies as a living sacrifice, holy and acceptable to God, which is your spiritual worship. Do not be conformed to this world, but be transformed by the renewing of your minds, so that you may discern what is the will of God—what is good and acceptable and perfect.

—Romans 12:1-2

Centuries ago, after the church had become centered and clustered within large cities, the movement began to develop a Christian way of life consisting of retreat, contemplation, and simple living. This was known as the monastic movement, and the men and women who devoted themselves to this new way were later called the desert fathers and mothers. Anthony, who lived around 350 CE, is often considered the father of monasticism.

While few modern Christians will take up this way of life, it is compelling to listen to some of these early teachings regarding simplicity and devotion to Christ. In many respects, our lives are no less contorted by the world these early monks encountered. For example, Anthony warned that the two main enemies of the spiritual life are anger and greed. Anger, he believed, emerges when we feel that we have been deprived of love, security, relationship, or hope. And if we searched our hearts, we would discover that what was true then is true now.

Likewise, Anthony believed that greed flows out of this anger. What we don't have, we want. And not just with money; greed can also take the form of being in possessive relationships, accruing security in things rather than principles, or even holding ourselves at the center of life.

It is not easy to get past these things—especially as we prepare for Christmas, with all of its buying, and gift-giving, and stark awareness of our blessings and deficiencies. In fact, this season can often exacerbate our anger and greed and make us less receptive to the very Christ we profess to welcome and celebrate.

Perhaps transformation is needed in the Advent journey toward Bethlehem. Perhaps we need to see things and people in new ways, to listen to the Spirit through new ears, to hear the cry of the needy as a cry of hope and salvation. During the days ahead, what transformations might be helpful to you and your family? Are there alluring temptations that need to be ignored? Are there sacrifices that need to be made to see Christ's love in new ways?

Prayer: *Lord, renew us and open our eyes, so that we can see past the allures and temptations of this season. We are often seduced by busyness and a frantic pace. Slow us down, Lord. Help us to find sanctuary and security in your loving embrace and the promises of your everlasting love. Amen.*

True Charity

I . . . beg you to lead a life worthy of the calling to which you have been called, with all humility and gentleness, with patience, bearing with one another in love, making every effort to maintain the unity of the Spirit in the bond of peace. There is one body and one Spirit, just as you were called to the one hope of your calling, one Lord, one faith, one baptism, one God and Father of all.

—EPHESIANS 4:1-6

In every generation, there are people who want to make a difference—people whose thoughts and great aspirations move the hearts and minds of the church. In 1856, in London, that person was William Booth, a Methodist who noted that, once again, people had become estranged from the church, and the church, subsequently, had become estranged from the needs of society. Despair and hopelessness had been wed to poverty and discord. There was no unity of service to meet the needs of humanity, and God seemed, to many, so distant and unkind.

Booth began organizing small bands, usually of trumpets, other horns, and drums, to play on the street corners during the days preceding Christmas—a time when many people might, as Charles Dickens had written in his novel *A Christmas Carol* more than a decade prior, "open their shut-up hearts" to others. Booth collected pocket change and began to address the wider needs of humanity with acts of *charity*—a word that, then, was deeply ingrained in the gospel proclamation of God's love in Christ as service and redemption to the world.

What happened then has continued to this day: Booth envisioned the formation of The Salvation Army—a people dedicated to advancing the Christian faith through education, the eradication of poverty, and to any act of charity that would meet the wider needs of humanity. Perhaps you too have participated in this movement without ever realizing the intent. And that was part of Booth's vision as well.

During this Advent season, our hearts tend to be more open to others, and we often acknowledge the poverty and needs of society. Likewise, our hearts are often moved to the needs that exist in our own families and in the lives of our friends and neighbors. Kindness swells, and so does the spirit of Christmas. True charity is any act that moves us deeper into the love of Christ or serves the needs of humanity—even basic ones such as food, clothing, or shelter. These acts remind us that Christ entered the world as a weak and vulnerable child, dependent upon others for his basic needs and for his growth and sustenance. His birth is an invitation for us to provide for his needs, which we see most clearly in the needs of others. For, as Jesus once said, "Just as you did it to one of the least of these who are members of my family, you did it to me" (Matt. 25:40).

How have you demonstrated charity in your celebration of Christmas? How are you preparing to see Christ or to welcome him through your actions today?

Prayer: *Gracious Lord, you came among us as a small and vulnerable infant. But you also came to serve and to give your life as a ransom for many. Bless the hands and feet that go forth to serve in your name, so that in all things, even our smallest acts of charity can be a greater demonstration of your abiding love. Amen.*

A New Day

Besides this, you know what time it is, how it is now the moment for you to wake from sleep. For salvation is nearer to us now than when we became believers; the night is far gone, the day is near. Let us then lay aside the works of darkness and put on the armor of light.

—ROMANS 13:11-12

When I was a child, I could, and frequently did, sleep for twelve hours or more at a crack. My body craved sleep. Mornings were difficult. But as I have grown older and my life has been overtaken by routines, work, and myriad obligations, I have discovered that I often have difficulty sleeping. Mornings are a welcome respite, a quiet time, before the frantic pace of the day begins. Mornings are beginnings—a kind of new creation, when it is possible to start over, leave the burdens of the previous day behind, and embrace all the possibilities that a new day presents.

I wonder if these are not some of the ideas behind the apostle Paul's writing to the church in Rome. Here, the apostle asks believers to leave behind the darkness, to embrace the light, and to awake from sleep—a metaphor used throughout the Bible for everything from apathy to death. He calls upon believers to recognize that God's salvation is near. These themes and ideas can come full circle as we journey through Advent.

Consider, for example, the many distractions that pervade our lives. It is often difficult to see God's helpfulness and interventions in our lives when our attentions are wrested away by worry, busyness, entertainment, disasters, fear, anxiety, or even the next big game on TV. When we move our attentions from these to cast our faith upon God, it can often be like awakening from sleep. The pall of darkness lifts. We see life in a new light.

As a child, I could never figure out why my parents enjoyed the mornings so much; but now that I am older, I think I know. It is because the mornings offer us the possibility of a new order, a new creation, a new way to think about our lives—our worries and concerns. Instead of dropping back to sleep in the darkness of yesterday, we can embrace new paths of gratitude, hope, or joy.

Today offers these possibilities and more. So, as you cast your faith into this new day, what do you see? What are you hoping for?

> **Prayer:** *Dear Lord, thank you for this new day. Yesterday is behind me. And I trust that you will walk with me through this day's possibilities, hopes, and challenges. I offer you my best, and I trust that you will forgive me when I fail and lift me when I fall. More than this, give me joy and gratitude for this day's wonders. Amen.*

Harmony

May the God of steadfastness and encouragement grant you to live in harmony with one another, in accordance with Christ Jesus, so that together you may with one voice glorify the God and Father of our Lord Jesus Christ. Welcome one another, therefore, just as Christ has welcomed you, for the glory of God.

—ROMANS 15:5-7

I have a friend who writes a popular series of novels about people in a fictional Indiana town called Harmony. Though lighthearted and hopeful, the novels deal, nevertheless, with the various trials, tribulations, and troubles experienced in this small town. Harmony, it seems, is anything but harmonious.

In many respects, our Advent preparations are attempts to bring ourselves, our homes, and our relationships into synergy. We attempt to align our better angels with the sights, sounds, and company of heaven. We spend time decorating, conversing, and preparing for God's intervention. And there is a spirit that exists in Advent that seems to enliven the generosities, joys, and helpfulness of humanity.

In short, there is a greater willingness, it seems, to embrace the possibilities God places before us—possibilities of hope, compassion, and joy.

There are new harmonies at play in this season.

The apostle Paul envisioned harmony as one of the attributes of the Christian life. And for him, harmony best played out in the manner in which we welcomed others and demonstrated the hospitality of God. Instead of seeing others as outsiders, Paul invited the Christian community to embrace everyone with the love of God—bringing them inside the gracious embrace of Creator God.

This is very much a part of our Advent preparations as we offer open houses, dinners, parties, and the warm hospitality of laughter and friendship. Congregations typically present children's and musical programs that encapsulate these invitations and offer them to the communities they serve.

This is the kind of harmony that draws others into God's household. And when we invite others to share in our common humanity—even recognizing that we all share the same struggles, difficulties, hopes, and dreams—we discover that we have more in common than we at first realized. We are more alike than different.

How might we demonstrate this harmony to others? What invitations might we offer that could warm the cold heart or embrace the lonely or the fearful? In demonstrating God's welcome, we bring the whole world into harmony through the grace of Jesus Christ.

Prayer: *Gracious God, thank you for welcoming me and for providing your hospitality through those who have touched my life and helped make me who I am. Help me now to be a source of welcome and hospitality to others—and lead me into those paths that are in harmony with your will and your ways. I thank you for the gifts of this day. Amen.*

ADVENT
Day 6

Looking for Signs

A shoot shall come out from the stump of Jesse,
and a branch shall grow out of his roots.
The spirit of the LORD shall rest on him,
the spirit of wisdom and understanding,
the spirit of counsel and might,
the spirit of knowledge and the fear of the LORD.
His delight shall be in the fear of the LORD.

—ISAIAH 11:1-3

A few years ago, I made a pilgrimage on the Camino de Santiago—the historic pilgrimage that millions of Christians and others have made over the centuries through northern Spain on the way to the traditional burial place of Saint James. The Camino is marked, for hundreds of miles, by signposts containing an image of a scallop shell. Official pilgrims on the journey also wear a scallop shell as they walk to indicate their destination and yearnings.

These signposts along the way are important markers. Often, when one encounters a fork in the trail or when walking through busy intersections of cities, it would be easy to lose one's way without these signs along the way.

All of us, at one time or another, have longed for signs from God. Sometimes we even pray for signs—for those clear and obvious indications that we are on the right path or that we are making the correct decision at some juncture in life. However, if we are honest with ourselves, we most commonly discover that God's signs are not obvious. They are not like signposts on a trail. God's signs are not lightning flashes or burning bushes. They are not miraculous interventions that pick us up or place us on another path.

The words of Isaiah the prophet may be of some comfort to us here. Isaiah envisioned God's sign as being embodied in one who would demonstrate the spirit of God, the delight of the Lord. *Wisdom, understanding, might* . . . concepts that might also help us as we journey through an Advent pilgrimage toward the one who we believe embodied these signs of God.

Asking God for signs to direct our way is not nearly as important as following the one *who is* God's sign—Jesus the Christ, the babe of Bethlehem. Like the shepherds of old, we might discover that God will direct us to the Lord when we are able to say, "Let us go now to Bethlehem and see this thing that has taken place" (Luke 2:15).

Indeed, Advent can be a time of hope and salvation. The Lord is our sign.

Prayer: *God of wonders, it seems I am always looking for the proper path through life. There are often detours and pitfalls, times I lose my way. But you continue to direct my paths as I look to Jesus—the pioneer and perfecter of my faith. I give thanks for the one who is the Way. Grant that today, I may follow him with new eyes and ears, for I know you will direct my path. Amen.*

From Fear to Faith

But the angel said to [the shepherds], "Do not be afraid; for see—I am bringing you good news of great joy for all the people: to you is born this day in the city of David a Savior, who is the Messiah, the Lord. This will be a sign for you: you will find a child wrapped in bands of cloth and lying in a manger."

—LUKE 2:10-12

Some years ago, I asked the members of my congregation to write down their fears and worries on postcards (anonymously) so that I could share them in a sermon. The results were insightful and, at times, astounding.

For example, people were honest in sharing fears that were pronounced and obvious to many: worries about deteriorating health, jobs, finances, parenting, relationships, and the environment. Other postcards indicated fears that were less obvious but perhaps more overwhelming: fears about death, overcoming depression, or feelings of uselessness or meaninglessness. And some people expressed surprising fears with regard to their search for ways they could better serve Christ and the church. Some feared that they had not yet found their places in God's kingdom work.

I wonder if those shepherds roaming along the hillsides near Bethlehem experienced some of those same fears when the angel announced the glad tidings of Christ's birth. Often, in the scriptures, we hear only about the fear itself—which we most commonly assume to be terror. But there are other fears that often surface when we find ourselves in the presence of God—or when grace suddenly or unexpectedly overwhelms us. We can wonder: *Why me?* or *How should I respond to or be responsible for this good news?*

Advent and our journey to Bethlehem can awaken these observations and questions within us. As we become aware of our fears, we can hand them over to God so that we can truly experience the grace God affords us. We can begin to live by faith, not by fear. The wonder of the Bethlehem journey is not only in the arrival; sometimes, the wonder can be revealed when we embrace the journey and decide to take a first step of faith, just like the shepherds. They had to be willing to leave behind their fears and their cares and step across the hills and valleys that were awaiting them on the way to Bethlehem. Our lives are no less fearful or arduous. We have our hills and valleys to navigate. But God has offered us the same good news: Come and see what God has done!

Prayer: *O Lord, it often seems that there are many obstacles between us. Some of these are not of my making. Others are barriers that I have placed there. Refresh my spirit and my faith today, and help me to set out on the path you have for me. Use me. Melt me. Mold me. And please remove my fears and replace them with faith. Amen.*

ADVENT

Day 8

Making Decisions

This is my prayer, that your love may overflow more and more
with knowledge and full insight to help you to determine what is
best, so that in the day of Christ you may be pure and blameless.

—Philippians 1:9-10

M y first year in seminary, I lived in a graduate student apartment complex with a student from China. That first week, as
we became acquainted with each other and the differences in our
cultures, customs, and cuisines, I began to realize that we were run-
ning low on food. Our fridge was nearly empty, and so, one morning, we walked a few blocks to a super-sized discount store to fill a
shopping cart.

When we entered the store, however, my friend seemed frozen
in his shoes, his mouth agape in wonder and awe. He appeared to be
overwhelmed. It took hours for me to walk him through the store,
as he seemed perplexed—overcome, even—by the shelves filled
with products and choices. Later, back at our apartment, I asked
him about the experience.

"I am not used to having so many choices," he told me. "I just couldn't seem to make a decision. I had never seen so many brands of toothpaste, so many selections and assortments. How could I choose from among so many?"

Over the years, I have thought much about this shopping experience with my friend, and I have realized that people can feel overwhelmed by life's many decisions. In fact, we have to make decisions every day. From the moment we rise in the morning to the moment we go to sleep, our days are filled with a dizzying assortment of decisions and alluring choices that can call to us at home, at work, in our relationships, in our commitments, and in our finances. Many people can, and do, feel overwhelmed, even stymied, by the choices they have to make. And then, some people may shut down entirely and make no choices at all. They seem to flit about on the winds of happenstance and chance.

The apostle Paul, in his letter from prison to the Philippians, offers another option for us. His invitation is that we allow love and knowledge to overflow in our lives to the point where we will have insight to determine what is best. Our decisions—even the seemingly small and insignificant ones—can have a large impact on our lives when they are made in faith, when we trust that a decision is best not just for us but for others too. Ultimately, it is God's love in the world that makes the difference through us.

Today, as you ponder the many choices you have to make—or perhaps as you create your to-do list—give some thought and prayer to what is best. Is there a conversation you need to have? Is there someone you need to visit? Is there an act of kindness you could offer? Is there a difficult decision you need to wrestle with or a gift you need to give?

The Advent journey is filled with such opportunities and decisions. While we are on our way with God and journeying toward Jesus, it is important to ponder what is best.

Make today your best day. Live it to the fullest and make each decision count.

> **Prayer:** Lord Jesus Christ, you made the decision to give yourself fully and freely, to enter this world and live among us in humility and love. Help me to respond today in gratitude and helpfulness as I make decisions large and small. I thank you for this day and its potential and promise. Amen.

Overcoming Adversity

I can do all things through him who strengthens me.

—Philippians 4:13

This simple verse from Philippians has been used (and abused) throughout the years. It has been used on posters and bumper stickers. Years ago, a friend insisted that this verse promised that we could accomplish anything if we believed in Jesus. "Anyone who believes could be president," he insisted, "or could become the best baseball player in history. Anyone can become a millionaire. Everyone can achieve his or her greatest dream." But is that what this promise is about? Is that what Paul is speaking about here—riches, fame, dreams, aspirations?

Looking at the full context of what Paul is describing in Philippians, it is helpful to note that Paul is describing hardships—difficulties and obstacles that are a part of every life. Paul is not speaking of outlandish dreams or oversimplified goals or our individual desires for personal achievement or fortune. He is addressing human suffering—and the strength God provides when we are at our lowest points. "Don't forget," Paul writes, "that Christ suffered too. His strength can help us to overcome the struggles we are facing. We can overcome with his help."

I believe that Paul was correct. God is "a very present help" in every time of trouble (Ps. 46:1). God is our strength and shield (see Psalm 28:7). God will not abandon us in our time of trial. Christ made this known when he said, "I am with you always" (Matt. 28:20). No doubt, during this season of darkness and turmoil, you have experienced your share of troubles and difficulties. Some of these may be health-related or financial or relational or spiritual. You may have had moments when you felt like giving up or when you felt terribly alone or terrified. But it can be comforting to remember these words: "I can do all things through him who strengthens me."

As you face today's adversities and challenges, breathe this thought in and offer it as a prayer. God is strong enough to give you hope and assurance. God's grace is enough.

And if Christ is for you, then who can be against you (see Romans 8:31)?

Prayer: *Dear God, I continue to wait for you expectantly. There is much to do today. Often, I am filled with doubt and despair. But I will lift up my faith today and trust in your strength. You will see me through. Amen.*

From Old to New

I am about to do a new thing;
now it springs forth, do you not perceive it?
I will make a way in the wilderness
and rivers in the desert.

—Isaiah 43:19

One of the most memorable and impactful Christmas presents I ever received was a small cassette tape recorder that my grandparents gave me when I was a young teen. I would sit for hours, recording music and making humorous gag reels—often playing these tapes back and listening to these recordings over and over again. I suppose this is one of the reasons why I continue to enjoy television reruns to this day. There is something comforting about the familiar situations, the humorous dialogue that can be recited from memory.

But there are also dangers in the familiar—in the reruns and rote conversations and situations we play back time and again in our minds. In life, these familiar places, these reruns of resentment, bitterness, victimization, pain, or low self-esteem, can leave us replaying the same choruses and situations over and over again. And we can seem to be stuck in place, immobilized with fear or heartache, unable to break free.

Over the years, I have known so many people who seem to be stuck. Some college students, for example, may hear the voice of a former teacher or coach telling them, "You are not smart enough." Or some married couples may hear a voice that tells them, "You cannot overcome this problem or build a future together." Older adults may hear the inner voice of a child telling them, "You have failed." There are many recordings we replay in our minds.

Centuries ago, the prophet Isaiah envisioned God doing a new thing—erasing the old perceptions of barrenness and scarcity and replacing them with fruitfulness and abundance. Isaiah envisioned what could be when we stop living in reruns and prerecorded attitudes and take on the vision of a new path, a fresh way, that God desires to give us. I wonder how rich and life-changing our old situations might become if we could see ourselves on God's new path. What might happen to us if our Advent journey to Bethlehem were a new way instead of a familiar one? What changes might God make in us?

This Advent, let's take a new step of faith instead of living in fear; or we might see God's abundance instead of our scarcity or God's blessings instead of our trepidation. Wonderful things can happen when we embrace something new, when we leave behind the old sorrows and exchange them for God's joys.

Prayer: *God of the new, I offer you my old ways—the conversations and situations I have often played back and allowed to pervade my life. I'm trading these for a new way—your way! Help me to take one new step today. And then another tomorrow. Amen.*

Fear Not!

"Do not be afraid, little flock, for it is your Father's good pleasure to give you the kingdom."

—LUKE 12:32

In the late 1990s, author Spencer Johnson wrote one of the best-selling self-help and business books of all time, the classic *Who Moved My Cheese?* It is a concise book—a parable of sorts—that offers an abundance of insights into personal decisions, business acumen, personal growth, and leadership. At one point, one of the mice characters in the parable asks the question, "What would you do if you weren't afraid?"[1]

This is really a gospel question—and one that Jesus posed time and again throughout his ministry. Jesus, it seems, was always trying to remind his followers that they should "fear not." As Jesus knew, fear is the greatest enemy of faith—for fear strangulates our ability to step out, to risk, to embrace the new, and to embrace others.

We fear so much in life. We fear our own inadequacies. We fear scarcity, pain, rejection. We often fear new situations, the unfamiliar, and people who aren't like us. And we can even fear God. According to Jesus, God wants to give us God's kingdom—and that's awfully big! When we hide away in fear, we deny or abandon the potentialities of God, the blessings and the joys God desires to give us. Instead of taking a risk and stepping out in faith, we often linger in our fears.

The Advent journey doesn't have to be this way. We can make decisions that are more faith-filled than fear-based. We can ride the crest of new blessings and joys. We can offer these to others too through our service and generosity.

Make today count for faith. Leave fear behind. Consider where and how the kingdom of God is being revealed in your blessings, your relationships, your work, your love, your life. And then, step into it.

You may experience more of God's kingdom than you ever knew.

Prayer: *Lord Jesus, thank you for reminding me that you are always by my side. I need not fear what I cannot see, for you are with me. I give you my fears today, and I replace them with faith. In your name, I pray. Amen.*

ADVENT
Day 12

Prepare

The beginning of the good news of Jesus Christ, the Son of God.
As it is written in the prophet Isaiah,

> *"See, I am sending my messenger ahead of you,*
> *who will prepare your way;*
> *the voice of one crying out in the wilderness:*
> *'Prepare the way of the Lord,*
> *make his paths straight.'"*

— MARK 1:1-3

During my middle-school years, I became an avid chess player. This was 1972, and the American Bobby Fischer had just defeated Boris Spassky of the Soviet Union to become the World Federation's World Chess Champion. Some of my friends and I spent hours at a time poring over the games Fischer and Spassky had played, analyzing various moves and strategies. I learned that chess is a game that can be described in phases—with a beginning, a middle game, and an endgame. But the beginning of a chess match is the most important, establishing the structure and power of the game that will be played through the middle and end.

The Gospel writers also used some of these ideas when writing their respective Gospels. Mark, in particular, is spare and concise in his presentation of Jesus—preferring to begin the story with an adult Jesus who, showing up on the scene mature and ready, is thrust into the spotlight after John the Baptist completes his ministry in the Judean countryside. John, as all of the Gospel writers agree, was sent in the power and place of Elijah the prophet to prepare the way for Jesus. John is setting the table for Jesus. But it is Jesus who will then be doing the heavy lifting and the full work of the kingdom of God. John the Baptist was the beginning—the preparation phase of the gospel—while Jesus would see the work through to the end.

That was the work then, but the work of the church now is to prepare hearts and minds to receive Jesus, to be his hands and feet and voice. Advent—with its many aspects of preparation and anticipation—is very much a season of readiness for greater things. It is why color and light and traditions play such a large part in our worship and festivities. It is why people more readily give, why there is a more generous spirit of sharing and helping. And in the anticipation of the new, people want to prepare themselves for something greater, for something new that God may do.

So—how do any of us prepare the way for Jesus?

We may have to jump in and begin. We may have to take some risks. We may have to put ourselves in a position of caring and helpfulness. It's getting ready; it's offering ourselves to God's work.

Prepare is a powerful word. It is a faith word. To prepare is to say to God: "I am available. Here I am, Lord. Send me."

Prayer: *O God, I'm often uncertain about how you can or will use me in your work. But I am willing. Today, I avail myself to your work. I am available. I am prepared. Use me, Lord. Amen.*

Landscaping

"Every valley shall be lifted up,
and every mountain and hill be made low;
the uneven ground shall become level,
and the rough places a plain."

—Isaiah 40:4

My congregation is loaded with master gardeners and, consequently, the landscaping around our facility is beautifully maintained. There are spring flowers and preparations made in all of our gardens and hedgerows. Summers are bright with color and rich greenery. And in the fall, our gardeners make sure that our grounds reflect the kind of welcome and hospitality that accompanies a well-thought-out migration to winter, with holly and evergreen adorning the entryways. I have always appreciated those people who have "green thumbs"—gifts for growing flowers and other plants and for seeing with heightened awareness, among the common landscapes and changing seasons, the new blessings of God. The richness of these gifts enlivens our sense of God's presence and invites us to an awareness of what God is doing.

Although I doubt the prophet Isaiah was a master gardener, he certainly was a visionary who saw evidence of God's spirit alive in the natural world. Low points on the horizon would be lifted. Mountains that could not be crossed would be made manageable. Rough would be made smooth. What insights these metaphors offer to us during the Advent season.

As we consider life's difficulties and challenges, we may lean into God's strength. As we ponder the seemingly insurmountable burdens of grief, poverty, or broken relationships, we may take solace in the promise that these mountains can be encountered and crossed. Or as we consider any dark time or any difficult experience we may face, it is helpful to know that these times will not last forever. God will see us through.

Perhaps, here, at the halfway journey of Advent, it is helpful to consider the landscape we have already navigated. As we look back upon our experiences, we can see that God has already seen us through much trouble and tribulation.

As Charles Wesley once wrote in his glorious hymn "And Are We Yet Alive," we too can sing the words,

> What troubles have we seen,
> What mighty conflicts past,
> Fighting without, and fears within,
> Since we assembled last!
>
> Yet out of all the Lord
> Hath brought us by his love;
> And still he doth his help afford,
> And hides our life above.[2]

Prayer: *Gracious God, you have been my help and salvation my whole life long—even before I was aware of your grace and guidance. Give me the strength and hope I will need to face and to manage the next array of obstacles and challenges in life. I face all of these and more knowing that you are with me and will never leave me. Amen.*

God's Time

*Do not ignore this one fact, beloved, that with the Lord one day
is like a thousand years, and a thousand years are like one day.*

—2 PETER 3:8

In April 2019, millions around the world watched as a massive fire consumed the interior of the Notre-Dame cathedral in Paris, France—a historic church that had stood for nearly a millennium and was, for many, a landmark and insignia of the Christian faith. Although first reports of the fire were largely pessimistic regarding the structure's survival, the limestone walls of the cathedral withstood the intense heat and will remain, with future repair work and rebuilding, as a sign of hope. Many artifacts and relics had been removed from the cathedral before the roof collapsed, providing a sense of relief for many around the world. But the cathedral itself also stood as a reminder of eternity—of the vastness of time and generations that have come and gone since the original construction on the church was completed.

We don't need millennia-old structures to remind us of time's relentless march, however. Every year, as we face the new beginnings in God's time and remember the old, we encounter the age-old conundrum of finding our place in the universe. Like the psalmist, we may be in awe of the grandeur of time itself and the rapidity with which life slips through our fingers. Or we may simply carry forward with a resolve that our time, like life itself, is in God's hands.

There is nothing wrong with acknowledging our own mortality—or the transient nature of life itself—as we yearn for the coming of Christ and his kingdom. After all, it is God's kingdom that we are praying for (not our own kingdoms); and when we acknowledge God's abiding presence over our mortality, we enter the timelessness of God—the One who has brought all things into existence and stands over and above time itself.

Thinking about such imponderable matters gives us patience, fortitude, and—ultimately—faith. We cannot give ourselves eternal life. We cannot give ourselves another day of life. We do not create our own experiences. All of these are gifts of God.

Today, as you ponder how far you have come and the dangers and trials that you have been spared, give thanks. Our lives are gathered up—have already been gathered up—into the timelessness of Eternal God. Thanks be to God.

Prayer: *Eternal God, I am in awe of your creation and the patience you show and the grace you offer. How can I ever thank you for these gifts? Help me to trust you today with these hours of my life, with the inexpressible gift of another day. In it and through it, I hope to live in such a way that will be pleasing to you, my Strength and my Redeemer. Amen.*

That's the Spirit!

The spirit of the Lord GOD is upon me,
because the LORD has anointed me;
he has sent me to bring good news to the oppressed,
to bind up the brokenhearted,
to proclaim liberty to the captives,
and release to the prisoners.

—ISAIAH 61:1

The first stirrings of my call to ministry were many years ago, when, as a nineteen-year-old college student, I began leading a Bible study and prayer service in the county jail. There, each week as I entered behind the bars and exited from them, I became increasingly aware of the power of the good news of Jesus—especially among those who are prisoners. Others, I noted, had become enslaved to or trapped in addictive behaviors such as drugs, alcohol, or theft.

There is a power in God's love—a power to heal and liberate.

John Wesley was one who believed that God loves us as we are. But God also loves us too much to allow us to remain as we are. Perhaps this is the spirit of the prophet Isaiah and also the spirit of Advent. We are always waiting on God to liberate us, to set us free, to make us more than we currently are. God is not through with any of us but is patient and willing to come alongside us in our brokenness and need.

How marvelous it is to reflect on these truths during a season of darkness and anticipation. Our goals and our needs are equally important to God, who is calling us forward into new light, new awareness, new creation, and new freedom. Today, spend some time reflecting on the many ways God has led you to new experiences and new moments—times, perhaps, when you have grown in faith or stretched your gifts and service outside your own comfort.

God is always doing a new thing; and, if we are willing, God will do a new thing in us today. We can step out, step up, and enter into a new place where God can heal us, free us, and offer us help and hope.

God can do that for others too—those we love, those we are praying for. Let that be our prayer today.

Prayer: *God of grace and glory, I bring before you my prayers for others today. Heal the hurt in those I love; and where I can help, bring me to their side. I offer myself today to your liberating spirit and the joy you can bring. Amen.*

Circumstantial Evidence

Rejoice always, pray without ceasing, give thanks in all circumstances; for this is the will of God in Christ Jesus for you.

—1 THESSALONIANS 5:16-18

Some years ago, when my wife and I were traveling through southern Ireland, we visited a beautiful cathedral in Galway. We marveled at the stained-glass windows, the high vaulted arches, the majestic organ perched in the chancel. But I was most enthralled by a large display in the nave of the cathedral—a colorful bulletin board that contained a myriad of prayers that had been written on index cards.

A cursory glance at some of these prayers made me aware of the deep gratitude the people of this community were experiencing. Despite circumstances of illness, difficulties, or distress, most people had written down prayers of gratitude for God's strength in hardship or thanksgiving for family, friendships, or hope through troubling times. The truth is, when we are experiencing difficulties, we often migrate toward feelings of despair or even wallow in self-pity. Gratitude is not an easy transition.

Despite his circumstances, centuries ago, the apostle Paul urged the new Christians in Thessalonika to gravitate toward prayers of thanksgiving. Paul did not say that suffering was the will of God, but he did urge the church to live in a spirit of joy and to offer continued gratitude to God. As many have discovered, our positive prayers have an impact not only on how we face life's difficulties but also on our outlook toward the future as well. Negativity has a tendency to breed feelings of helplessness, depression, and individuality. Positive thoughts and gratitude have a tendency to ingratiate us with others and help us to focus life and energies beyond ourselves. In short, a prayer of thanksgiving brings us a deeper awareness of God's love and helps us to live in harmony with ourselves and with others.

Perhaps there are prayers of gratitude that you might place on your private bulletin board today. These might be prayers of thanksgiving despite difficult circumstances or perhaps prayers that can help you note the support of God's people—or maybe even prayers of thanks for family and friends who have come alongside you over the years.

Advent is a beautiful season of anticipated joy, and our prayers can be a wonderful addition to our preparation to receive God's greatest gift: Jesus, the Christ.

> **Prayer:** *God, today I'm going to say, "Thank you." I could name my difficulties today or even the circumstances that often bring me down—but I'm going to look up, and I'm going to lift up. I will note your blessings. I will give thanks for the incredible gift of Jesus and his love. Amen.*

Restoration

When the LORD restored the fortunes of Zion,
*   we were like those who dream.*
Then our mouth was filled with laughter,
*   and our tongue with shouts of joy;*
then it was said among the nations,
*   "The LORD has done great things for them."*

—PSALM 126:1-2

My wife enjoys finding rustic furniture—pieces that have been heavily used and bruised—and restoring them to life via new glue, sanding, and refinishing. Many pieces in our home have been recovered from dank basements, dirty barns, or estate sales. My wife has an eye for discovering these diamonds in the rough and imagining how they might look fully restored or where a piece might fit into one of our rooms or add beauty to an otherwise drab and barren wall. Every time I glance at one of these old pieces of furniture—now made beautiful—I am reminded that God has always been in the restoration business.

When Abraham and Sarah are languishing in a far country, God promises to restore their name and give them a future through a promised child and to bring them to a new land. Later, God restores the Hebrew people by leading them out of slavery to freedom. The prophets demand restoration when the people of Israel and Judah are carried away into captivity. And there are other leaders, such as Nehemiah, who lead the people in restoring city walls and rebuilding the Temple. Later, the apostles proclaim that, through Jesus, we too can be restored and remade, day-by-day, into the image of our Creator, fully restored by the grace of Jesus Christ.

Indeed, Advent is a restoration season.

During these weeks preceding Christmas, we restore color and beauty to our homes, we cast light into darkened corners, and we restore our spirits with song and mirth. As Christians, there is a growing awareness for us that a new year is approaching as Advent begins and, with it, new promises of grace and goodness. God is always at work restoring.

Today, you might take note of these hopes and dreams. Perhaps you can consider the broken places that need to be mended, the lackluster that can be brightened, the rough edges of life that need to be made smooth. That is God's work. God's business. And today can be the day of restoration.

Prayer: *Gracious God, there is much work to be accomplished in me. I am not all I can be or all I want to be. But by your grace, I pray that I can take note of the great things you have done for me—the restorative work that you have already accomplished in me. And where I am still lacking, let the new work be accomplished. Amen.*

A Mystery

Now to God who is able to strengthen you according to my gospel and the proclamation of Jesus Christ, according to the revelation of the mystery that was kept secret for long ages but is now disclosed.

—ROMANS 16:25-26

I write mystery novels and stories under a *nom de plume.* I enjoy writing mysteries—in the classical sense—because there is something wonderful and exciting about discovery, about a wonderful outcome that is revealed only after an adventure into the unknown. The apostle Paul used this term *mystery* often in his epistles—citing that there are many aspects of our faith and proclamation that are currently hidden from our experience. The work of God is a mystery, Paul says, that was revealed through Jesus. In Christ, we can glimpse the formerly unseen ways God was working to redeem the world. Christ reveals these mysteries of God—offering us a glimpse into God's heart and grace and love.

Perhaps this sense of mystery is what makes this season so fun and engaging, particularly for children. Gifts are boxed and wrapped and placed under the tree. They can be seen, but the contents remain unknown until unwrapping. There are also family gatherings and traditional events that offer their sense of anticipation—and the yet-unknown outcomes produced by reunion and sharing. And there are expectations that go unfulfilled but must wait until some future time to be fully revealed to us.

Mystery is what is being described as faith in Hebrews: "the assurance of things hoped for, the conviction of things not seen" (11:1); or "For in hope we were saved. Now hope that is seen is not hope. For who hopes for what is seen?" (Rom. 8:24).

Today can be a day of mystery too. Embrace that hope and try to live in the unseen miracles of living by faith. It is not just the things we see that produce our experiences and our character but also those things we hope for and that remain beyond our understanding. Let the mysteries of this season produce more joy and wonder in your life and in the lives of those you love.

Prayer: O God, how marvelous are your ways. And how wondrous is your love. Help me to grapple with these mysteries today as I avail myself to you and to the needs of others. Help me to walk by faith today and to see in Jesus the mysterious beauty of your image and redemption. Amen.

Greetings

In the sixth month the angel Gabriel was sent by God to a town in Galilee called Nazareth, to a virgin engaged to a man whose name was Joseph, of the house of David. The virgin's name was Mary. And he came to her and said, "Greetings, favored one! The Lord is with you."

—LUKE 1:26-28

Robert Fulghum, whose book *All I Really Need to Know I Learned in Kindergarten* was a mainstay on the bestseller list in the early 1990s, tells about a discovery he made one summer day in his attic. Inadvertently, he discovered a box of old Christmas cards—including letters and family photos—that had languished, unread, in the attic heat. Removing the box that morning, Fulghum spent the rest of that summer day opening this lost Christmas mail, and he reveled in these reminders of the love that came down from heaven.

In Fulghum's experience, these greetings were even more powerful when removed from their usual context. Reading the greetings that summer day, he began to feel the new stirrings of promise and hope. The joy he felt was even more pronounced, the love of his family and friends made all the more real.

I wonder if this is not how Mary felt when she received the greeting from the angel Gabriel. This greeting was unexpected, had no prior context, and was simply an announcement that she had been favored by God and that God was with her to accomplish a great work.

Mary was the first to receive the good news that Christ would be born, just as the women at the tomb were the first to receive the good news of his resurrection. And that's part of the gospel, that God reaches us and abides in us through unexpected times and circumstances. God can accomplish a great work even when—and perhaps especially when—we are not expecting God to show up!

So, here we are in our season of wonder—a time when we commonly expect to hear about Jesus, when we are preparing hearth and home to receive him. But what if we could carry God's greeting with us into the New Year, into unexpected times and places? What if we were surprised by the joy of God's greeting—like Christmas cards received on a summer day—when we needed that reminder the most?

Today could be such a day.

If we look and listen closely, we might discover some nuance of God's abiding presence, God's announcement of good news in Jesus, that we had not known before.

Prayer: O Lord, I am often distracted by the busyness and hurried pace of my life. Most often, my attention is wrested away from your greeting, and I chase after other alluring sights and sounds. Help me to hear your greeting today and, like Mary, find a willingness to embrace the work you have for me to accomplish. I give you thanks for such grace, and I am emboldened to share your love today. Amen.

Family Life

Ascribe to the LORD, O families of the peoples,
ascribe to the LORD glory and strength.

—PSALM 96:7

Journaling has been a mainstay in my life for many years. There, in those small notebooks, I have written down experiences and observations. And at other junctures, I have made lists of lessons learned, asterisks or numbers that remind me to pay attention and to incorporate these lessons into life.

One observation that I return to—especially in more recent years—is the realization of how delicate life is and how quickly life can turn on a dime, for good or bad. And as loved ones have aged or died, there is an ever-widening awareness in my mind of how precious life is.

This is especially true of family.

I like to remind families—especially in times of grief and loss—that God not only created us as individuals but as families. And the psalmist echoes these sentiments often.

Advent is a time when we are especially aware of our family ties—the legacies and love that embrace us in strong relationship and common care. Many families have their traditions of the season. Some travel great distances to be together, while others mark the days reminiscing or exchanging gifts.

All of these and more serve to remind us that God has given us the gift of family and that we can, whenever we gather together, give thanks to God for these familial gifts. All of the families of the earth are precious to the Lord. None of our commitments and loves go unnoticed by the Creator of heaven and earth.

This year, take some moments to create your own family list. Write down some of the blessings you have experienced as a family. List the strengths that hold you together.

As with those of old, God is most concerned for our relationships with one another. Family—and becoming a family of God—is how we discover that we can accomplish more together than we can individually. Being and becoming a family of God is what the kingdom of God is like.

So, give thanks. Ascribe to the Lord strength and honor. Bless the Lord, and ask the Lord to bless your family.

Prayer: *O God, thank you for my family and for all ties of faith and love that strengthen me in times of distress and hardship. I ask for your blessing today. And I ask that my family may be a blessing to others. Amen.*

ADVENT
Day 21

Wake-up Call

"Keep awake therefore, for you do not know on what day your Lord is coming."

—MATTHEW 24:42

Perhaps, like me, you don't trust alarm clocks, especially when you are traveling and staying in a hotel. When I'm traveling, I always prefer to get a wake-up call from the front desk. A wake-up call is doubly important if much is at stake.

There have been many times in my life when I have slept through important meetings or missed deadlines or arrived late because I was not prepared. Staying awake, being aware, is an important aspect of faith.

We are especially aware of the importance of staying alert when we are taking an important journey. We do not want to fall asleep at the wheel, nor would we want to appear sleepy during an important job interview or a presentation.

Likewise, when we feel that God is asking us to do something important or we feel God's call to serve or to help others, we want to be at our best. Just as we would want to give our best to our boss or company, we should offer no less to God. Faith is what keeps us alive and awake, and when we freshen our faith through service and dedication to the things of God, we are made all the bolder and more vibrant in our abilities to focus on the tasks God has laid before us.

Today, give your best effort when you help a neighbor or when you are listening to someone who is looking for advice or a confidant. Staying fresh and alert is just another way of remaining hopeful and faithful in our journey with God.

Prayer: *Creator God, keep me fresh and enliven me with your energy and Spirit today. Help me always to be aware of your presence with me—no matter what I am doing or where I am going. Embolden me in the ways that make for love, peace, and reconciliation with others. In Christ's name, I pray. Amen.*

Planting Trees

A shoot shall come out from the stump of Jesse,
and a branch shall grow out of his roots.
The spirit of the Lord shall rest on him,
the spirit of wisdom and understanding,
the spirit of counsel and might,
the spirit of knowledge and the fear of the Lord.

—Isaiah 11:1-2

Trees occupy a special place in the scriptures—among the prophets and psalms and Gospels, especially—as a metaphor for the kingdom of God. The righteous were regarded as trees planted beside the life-giving water (see Psalm 1:3). Jesus used the tree to represent faith and the presence of the kingdom of God, and he spoke of faith the size of a mustard seed that could move a mountain (see Luke 17:6). And the prophet Isaiah imagined a tree stump that would sprout new life, a leader who would embody the very Spirit of God (see Isaiah 11:1-2).

In the days of Jesus, the palm tree was the symbol of Jewish identity and independence. Throughout the centuries, many Jewish and Christian leaders have used the metaphor of the tree to speak of a faith that looks to the future. Martin Luther, the leader of the Reformation in the sixteenth century, is considered to have said, "Even if I knew the world was going to end tomorrow, I would still plant an apple tree."

Trees, of course, actually live much of their life underground. The roots go deep. And most of the vitality of the earth and the rain is drawn up through the roots into the living thing.

The same is true of the human spirit. The struggles we have, the unseen forces we wrestle with, the thoughts and ideas that give shape to our lives go largely unseen. It is by faith that we embrace a future with confidence, asking that the spirit of Christ might rest upon us and guide us.

The metaphor of the tree invites us to consider our faith: From where are we drawing our strength? How deep are we willing to go to find a new vitality or a new direction in our lives? Are we more comfortable living shallow lives or are we made stronger through adversity and the challenge of difficult situations? These are great questions for us to ponder during Advent.

The tree offers us much to consider in these times. And perhaps through it, we may discover that our faith draws us into the spirit and counsel of God.

Prayer: *Creator God, as you have made all things, I know you are still creating in me too. You are not finished working on me. Thank you for your patience throughout the seasons of my life, and I pray that I may offer beauty, comfort, relief, joy, and strength to those I encounter today. Help me to rely upon your counsel through all of the adversity of my life. Amen.*

Getting Ready

*In those days John the Baptist appeared in the wilderness of
Judea, proclaiming, "Repent, for the kingdom of heaven has
come near." This is the one of whom the prophet Isaiah spoke
when he said,*

> *"The voice of one crying out in the wilderness:*
> *'Prepare the way of the Lord,*
> *   make his paths straight.'"*

—MATTHEW 3:1-3

Some years ago, when my wife and I were traveling through
Dublin, Ireland, we decided to see the Book of Kells, a ninth-
century ornamental, illustrated manuscript of the four New
Testament Gospels in Latin, which was on display at Trinity
College. We had no idea how long this bit of sightseeing would
take, but we made our way from our hotel to the campus, followed
signs, and eventually took our place at the end of a long queue. We

had no idea where the line was leading, nor how long it was, but in time, as we snaked slowly through hallways and anterooms, we began to see additional displays.

Most of these displays were designed to offer background explanation and history on the Book of Kells. There were explanations about the ancient parchments used, the luminaries who were believed to have written the manuscript, and much more. All of these displays, of course, were merely precursors to the actual Book of Kells itself. They were there to explain and to prepare us for what, we believed, we would eventually see at some point farther down the line.

It is interesting to note that all of the Gospel writers use these same devices and preparations in telling the story of Jesus. Each one begins the gospel message by telling us about John, who served as a sign, an envoy who would prepare the way for the arrival of Jesus. Each one notes—especially Matthew—that John was serving as the last in the line of prophets, those whose voices who had come before Jesus.

It is always difficult for us to approach Jesus this way, however. We prefer a direct line, a quick entrance through a side door. No waiting.

But the gospel actually begins with waiting, preparation, and repentance. That is, in part, what Advent is asking us to do: Get ready. Form a line. Take another step of faith. And then, when Jesus arrives on the scene, we will be fully prepared.

The idea of forming a queue—a church standing in a long line of witnesses and voices—is remarkable, when we think about it. We are marching through time, but we are also seeing Jesus—each in our own way—as for the first time.

Perhaps, as Advent draws to a close, we may feel that we have come some distance in our spirit. We may have lived more fully in love or showered others in generosity or gratitude. Or we may have found new reasons to trust or have given over some need or problem to God's grace and healing.

But whatever our experience, it is satisfying and replenishing to consider that waiting is always part of the journey too. At the end, we do see Jesus, for he is the goal.

Prayer: *Dear Jesus, help me to seek you, to wait for you, to take steps toward you today. I may not see the end of the journey clearly, but I am taking another step of faith today. Bless me and guide me in your path. Amen.*

Mary's Song

"My soul magnifies the Lord,
and my spirit rejoices in God my Savior,
for he has looked with favor on the lowliness of his servant.
Surely, from now on all generations will call me blessed."

—LUKE 1:46-48

Mary occupies a special place in our preparations for and anticipation of Jesus—and her song in Luke 1 is filled with joy, gratitude, humility, and grace. All of these attributes and more could be used to describe Mary's response to the angelic announcement that she would be the mother of the Lord.

Songs too occupy a special place in our celebrations. The traditional "Happy Birthday to You" song is probably one of the most ubiquitous tunes sung throughout the year. And most everyone has a favorite song or a favorite hymn.

Mary's song has also served as the inspiration for hundreds of other songs throughout the centuries. Charles Wesley wrote many hymns for the Methodist people based upon the song of Mary, including

"Come, Thou Long Expected Jesus." Other hymns, such as "Hail to the Lord's Anointed," "Away in a Manger," and "What Child Is This?" contain language and themes provided by Mary's response.

Mary's song also enlists our emotions and responses. How do we respond to unexpected news—especially outcomes that involve our struggle or willingness to submit to God's greater good? How might we feel about being asked to assume some great work for the Lord? Would we be elated? sad? anxious? Or might we have emotions of gratitude and joy, even if we couldn't see the end?

Mary's song invites us to ask such questions about our own faith but also to be thankful for Mary's humility and willingness to offer herself to God's plan.

Wending our way through Advent, we eventually begin to see the lights of Bethlehem and the distant gleam of a greater holy city. Our songs arise as we enter into the journey itself, a journey of faith and calm assurance that God moves with us along the way and that, by God's grace, we shall safely arrive.

When we make ourselves available to God, but also give thanks for those who have come before us and given us the faith, we do see that, as the writer of Hebrews describes, we are part of a great cloud of witnesses (see Hebrews 12:1).

Who knows, we might even break out in song ourselves.

Prayer

What can I give him, poor as I am?
If I were a shepherd, I would bring a lamb;
If I were a Wise Man, I would do my part;
Yet what I can I give him: give my heart.

—Christina G. Rosetti, "In the Bleak Midwinter"

ADVENT

Day 25

Patience

Be patient, therefore, beloved, until the coming of the Lord.

—James 5:7

Nearly fifteen years ago, when we moved into our current residence, my wife and I planted an assortment of fruit trees on our property. We set in apple and pear, cherry and peach, among others. Initially, we spent much time tending to the young orchard—fertilizing, watering, pruning as needed. But over time, we came to rely upon the good graces of nature itself—the wind and the rain and the elements—to further these trees toward maturity.

Patience—which is one of the hallmarks of the Christian faith—is not necessarily an easy virtue to acquire, nor it is necessarily easy to comprehend.

Patience, as described in the book of James, is not an acquiescence to fate or a slothful waiting for God to turn things around, nor even a waiting game—but a confident attitude and activity that makes us participants in the kingdom of God.

Patience comes to mind whenever I see a tree—especially one I planted years before. I am reminded of the hard work that was enlisted in the thing itself, the work of tending and supporting. I am reminded of all that was out of my control but worked for the good to bring about the growth and maturity. And I am reminded of the gifts of God that make all of life possible.

This is patience, I believe: the confident reminder that God is always at work, bringing our lives to maturity, helping us grow up and grow into a deeper awareness of Christ. Patience produces faith, which produces hope.

During this Advent season, perhaps you have hoped for many outcomes. This season reminds us that patience is not its own reward but a deeper faith that helps us see into the future God has in store for us.

It is the same patience that we reflect upon at the Communion Table when we affirm, "Christ has died, Christ is risen, Christ will come again."

All of time—the alpha and omega, the beginning and the end—is bound up in God's great love and redemption. We pray for the kingdom to come, for God's will to be done. This is patience at its finest.

Or as the prophet Isaiah once proclaimed, "Those who wait for the LORD shall renew their strength, they shall mount up with wings like eagles" (40:31).

Prayer: *"Our Father which art in heaven, Hallowed be thy name. Thy kingdom come, Thy will be done in earth, as it is in heaven. Give us this day our daily bread. And forgive us our debts, as we forgive our debtors. And lead us not into temptation, but deliver us from evil: For thine is the kingdom, and the power, and the glory, for ever. Amen."*
—Matthew 6:9-13, KJV

Signs of Life

When John heard in prison what the Messiah was doing, he sent word by his disciples and said to him, "Are you the one who is to come, or are we to wait for another?" Jesus answered them, "Go and tell John what you hear and see: the blind receive their sight, the lame walk, the lepers are cleansed, the deaf hear, the dead are raised, and the poor have good news brought to them. And blessed is anyone who takes no offense at me."

—MATTHEW 11:2-6

When I was a seminary student, I endured a semester in a large university hospital serving as a chaplain. This was one of the most challenging times in my life, when faith and fortitude were tested in a crucible of pain and suffering. I was also challenged to learn the various "codes" that the doctors and other hospital staff used over the intercom to indicate particular emergencies or needs. Sometimes, I was the one called upon to visit a patient or console a grieving family.

One weekend, I was helping a family in the emergency room when a nurse beckoned me to the corner and whispered to me that the person who had just come in by ambulance had arrived DOA—which meant "Dead on Arrival."

When receiving such a word, it is difficult to think about "signs of life"—the hopeful presence of God.

But that is precisely what Jesus asks John to look for as the signs of the kingdom of God. Jesus speaks to many conditions here: people who have closed their ears to the world's needs and suffering, perhaps, but who discover newfound compassion and energies for service; others who have died—inside and out—but are suddenly raised up in new life and faith; or others who have been ostracized or excluded from the community yet discover that they are accepted and embraced by those who see in them the gifts of God.

God is still showing us signs of life, if we want to look for them.

Perhaps you can reflect on those times and situations where you felt hopeless or estranged, only to discover that God was with you all along. Or perhaps you have experienced these new signs of life as you have witnessed the hopeful progress of others or been allowed to be a source of blessing to another person.

Regardless, the season preceding Christmas offers us these and many other opportunities for service, reflection, and helpfulness. And in so doing, we may discover that our eyes or ears are opened too—and perhaps we will see Jesus more clearly than we have ever seen him before.

Prayer: *Dear Jesus, I am going to look for you today. I'm going to find your face in those who suffer or feel pain. I am going to listen for your voice in the shrill cry of the child or the silence of the old. And I am going to serve you through those I meet today—as I will call them your children. Amen.*

ADVENT
Day 27

Rescued

Then we will never turn back from you;
give us life, and we will call on your name.
Restore us, O Lord God of hosts;
let your face shine, that we may be saved.

—Psalm 80:18-19

A sign on the ship read: Life Preserver Found Under Seat. I wondered how many people had paused to consider the sign or feel under the seat . . . just in case.

We often speak of salvation in the Christian faith, and, interestingly enough, the root of this word in the Greek language (*sozo*) is akin to throwing a life preserver to a drowning person. To be saved is to be rescued; it is being pulled into life, not slipping under the waves.

The psalmist speaks often of this salvation. As we approach the end of Advent and turn our attentions to the celebrations of Christmas, let us pause and consider this salvation that was, in fact, the good news proclaimed by angels and shepherds, by both the high and the humble. The proclamation of God's salvation in Jesus Christ is a bold one—a gospel filled with hope, forgiveness, and assurance.

Often, in life, we find ourselves in the midst of a storm. We feel swallowed up by waves of grief or oceans of despair. We sink in life's alarms.

But the babe of Bethlehem is an invitation, a declaration: God is with us. And where there is the spirit of the Lord, there is hope and salvation.

Consider what salvation means to you. How has God delivered you from despair and death? Where have you enjoyed the blessings of God's abiding presence, the calm assurance that God is walking with you—even through the valley of death? Who or what has been a life preserver to you?

This season offers us much time for reflection and introspection. There is joy.

We have been rescued!

Prayer: *God with Us . . . how wondrous is the miracle of salvation—which is none other than your abiding presence with us, assuring us of forgiveness and hope. Thank you for these precious reminders of your love and especially for the gift of a Savior: Christ the Lord. Amen.*

ADVENT
Day 28

God with Us

CHRISTMAS EVE

Now the birth of Jesus the Messiah took place in this way. When his mother Mary had been engaged to Joseph, but before they lived together, she was found to be with child from the Holy Spirit. Her husband Joseph, being a righteous man and unwilling to expose her to public disgrace, planned to dismiss her quietly. But just when he had resolved to do this, an angel of the Lord appeared to him in a dream and said, "Joseph, son of David, do not be afraid to take Mary as your wife, for the child conceived in her is from the Holy Spirit. She will bear a son, and you are to name him Jesus, for he will save his people from their sins." All this took place to fulfill what had been spoken by the Lord through the prophet:

> *"Look, the virgin shall conceive and bear a son*
> *and they shall name him Emmanuel,"*

which means, "God is with us."

—MATTHEW 1:18-23

Over the years, I have encountered many people in need. Some have a need for necessities, such as food or lodging. Others are looking for answers to life's problems. Still others may need something as simple as transportation to a doctor's appointment or a few dollars for a bus ticket. But common to our human predicament is a need for relationship. Help comes from others. Hope is never found in isolation.

Loneliness and isolation are the most despairing of circumstances, however, and yet many people find it difficult to articulate their need for community and relationship.

Perhaps we all do.

The story of Christ's birth actually begins with these human experiences of isolation and despair. Joseph felt this way when he learned Mary was pregnant. Fear overtook him. He felt rejected. Alone.

But the first word of the gospel is Fear not! And then the subsequent word is an old affirmation: *Emmanuel*—"God is with us"!

Wonderful things happen to us—inside and out—when we realize that we are not alone. And when we realize that God is with us, life changes.

The message of Christmas is an invitation to enter into relationship with God through the gift of Jesus—who enters the human predicament, our human experiences, in order to show us God's love and redeem us from sin and death. This relationship is simple and yet profound.

Christmas is a reminder that we are invited into the community of God's love, into the embrace of God's presence. No longer do our lives have to be defined by isolation, despair, and loneliness—God has come near!

Jesus is Emmanuel.

Prayer: *Emmanuel, I am grateful for your abiding presence with me and for the calm assurance you provide during times of fear and anxiety. You have walked my path—experienced the same pain, the same hardships. Thank you for entering my life and for understanding my predicament and offering me your grace. In your holy name, I pray. Amen.*

CHRISTMAS

A CHRISTMAS PRAYER

We may still see the ancient face
Of king and shepherd in ourselves
Or perhaps in delving deeper
A migration of the fear
Where a high hope dwells
Ever near
In the riches of God's grace.

CHRISTMAS DAY

Wonder

In that region there were shepherds living in the fields, keeping watch over their flock by night. Then an angel of the Lord stood before them, and the glory of the Lord shone around them, and they were terrified. But the angel said to them, "Do not be afraid; for see—I am bringing you good news of great joy for all the people: to you is born this day in the city of David a Savior, who is the Messiah, the Lord. This will be a sign for you: you will find a child wrapped in bands of cloth and lying in a manger." And suddenly there was with the angel a multitude of the heavenly host, praising God and saying,

> *"Glory to God in the highest heaven,*
>   *and on earth peace among those whom he favors!"*

When the angels had left them and gone into heaven, the shepherds said to one another, "Let us go now to Bethlehem and see this thing that has taken place, which the Lord has made known to us."

—LUKE 2:8-15

Many of us embrace Christmas Day as a mark of tradition and faith. We assume that we are drawn to Christ because our faith compels us or because our histories dictate that our understanding of Jesus remains steadfast and unchanging.

But the announcement of Christ's birth and the response of the shepherds was quite different from what we might assume. In fact, the shepherds' questions and their inquisitive response to the angelic announcement is more akin to our times than we might realize. As we think about it, most people are drawn to Jesus because of their questions rather than their certainty. Like the shepherds, they want to go and see if Jesus fulfills some longing or hope in their lives. They wonder how Jesus might help them through times of crisis or despair.

When my children were younger, I can recall having some of these conversations about Jesus on Christmas Day. My children asked questions such as, "Why was Jesus born?" "Who was he?" "Why wasn't he born in a hospital?" "Why was Jesus born like us?"

These are questions—as well as many others—that people have asked through the ages. It is a wonder that has drawn saints and theologians to Bethlehem and causes us, even today, to ponder these deeper questions about Jesus—along with a fair number of questions the Bible doesn't seem to answer about him.

This Christmas, we might do well to recover some of that childhood wonder and ask our questions. We might have a family conversation amid the usual traditions that offer a safe place to ponder our own doubts and fears—and ultimately the questions that have drawn us to Jesus in the first place.

Wonder is, perhaps, the most important ingredient in a vital faith. Without a sense of wonder and an inquisitive spirit, our faith can wither and die.

We stop believing when we stop asking questions.

So, let us go and see. We might discover something new in our questions and our wonder that will make Jesus all the more real to us.

Prayer: Lord Jesus, I have so many questions about you. In many ways, I'm still trying to get to know you, Lord, and I'm still on the way to Bethlehem, just like the shepherds. Increase my wonder. Help me to remain inquisitive and surprised by joy at new turns. Give me grace to find you and see you in the questions as well as the answers. Let this Christmas Day be filled with a sense of delight and unexpected wonder. In your name, I pray. Amen.

SECOND DAY
of Christmas

Ancestry

For a child has been born for us,
a son given to us;
authority rests upon his shoulders;
and he is named
Wonderful Counselor, Mighty God,
Everlasting Father, Prince of Peace.

—Isaiah 9:6

Last year for Christmas, my wife received an Ancestry DNA kit. It is one of those popular packages that enable individuals to trace their lineage and, in some cases, discover a family line they did not know they had or relatives who were unbeknownst to them. It seems that ancestry research is one of the most popular trends among younger people—and it is especially revealing for those who have been displaced or felt removed from their family history or their awareness of the past. A DNA test can reveal hidden passageways and relationships, connections that unite us to recent and distant history.

The celebrations of Christmas, while focusing on the birth of Jesus, can actually take us back much further—to a time when prophets and teachers envisioned a coming messiah or anointed leader who would lead the people (as Moses had done generations before) from bondage to freedom. Others envisioned a great king in the line of David—another hero from the past. And still others believed the messiah would be a great teacher or orator who would speak the words of God.

In all ages, people have longed to have connections with the divine, with God who created the whole human family. The Bible, one might say, is a spiritual genealogy—a history of our familial connections that unite us together in faith.

The prophet Isaiah envisioned a great leader, a Messiah, who would be none other than God—a Counselor, a Prince, but also, a present friend and helper whose authority and power would be unequaled.

But we don't have to trace our spiritual lineage back to first-century Judea to feel connected to Jesus. This is a gift we receive by faith. In Christ, we are told, we become spiritual heirs, sisters and brothers, bound together in his one body—the church.

Perhaps Christmas is one of the most cherished of seasons because we do become more acutely aware of these spiritual ties— these friendships and caring bonds that make us a family.

Christmas is a good time to give thanks for the church—the family of God.

Prayer: *God of all peoples, how wonderful are these thoughts of being spiritual heirs of Jesus. I am grateful that I am joined to him and to so many others who claim his name. I pray for the church today, for pastors and leaders and all who serve. I pray for those who have entrusted the church to me, and I ask that I may cherish these friendships and mark them as some of the deepest blessings in my life. In Jesus' name, I pray. Amen.*

THIRD DAY
of Christmas

Hope

Say among the nations, "The LORD is King!
The world is firmly established; it shall never be moved.
He will judge the peoples with equity."

—PSALM 96:10

I grew up in a small town, and the most powerful person I knew as a child was the president of the town council. My world was not populated by either influential or wealthy people. It was years later before I attended events to hear speeches by politicians or would be made privy to the ideas proffered by celebrities or internationally known individuals.

My hunch is that most of us have grown up in a world like this—a world where our understanding of power is not someone far off in the distance, with respect more commonly given to parents, elder family members, and high-profile friends. In short, for many of us, the idea of a "king" would be more akin to something out of a fairy tale than real life.

Still, we all long for the idea of a heavenly power—one who can sort out the inequalities of this life and somehow bring new balance and order to the world in which we live. We long for justice and peace.

Christmas is such a time to dream this dream.

Christmas is an opportunity for us to turn our attention and faith to the Sovereign of the universe, the one who can restore not only our personal lives but also the larger order (and disorder) of life. Only God can accomplish this.

During Christmas, we also see how the world is swept up in some semblance of peacemaking and peacebuilding. There is an opportunity for the leaders of the world to make progress toward reconciliation, justice, and hope for all people. And often, there are attempts to bring these high and lofty aspirations to the table of nations, a renewed hope for some lasting peace.

Jesus has often been described in such ways: the Prince of Peace, the Way, the Truth. These are just a few of the names associated with Jesus, who came to build a bridge between humanity and God.

In these days of longing, let us not forget the big dreams, the seemingly overwhelming obstacles that need to be addressed in our world. God still reigns. The universe belongs to the One who made it. We are not abandoned.

There is hope.

Prayer: *Gracious God, I often fall into despair and feel limited by the small, confined dreams of the individual. But help me to see what you are doing in the world around me. You are working in the hearts and minds of your children to bring about justice, reconciliation, and peace. Help me to be a part of this work. Help me to do what I can. The rest belongs to you, O God. Amen.*

FOURTH DAY
of Christmas

Count Your Blessings

*I will recount the gracious deeds of the LORD,
the praiseworthy acts of the LORD.*

—ISAIAH 63:7

When I was a teenager, I enjoyed serving as our congregation's Sunday school secretary. It was my job to make the rounds to the various classes, take attendance, and record these numbers in a ledger. I also displayed each week's total attendance on a display board that was positioned in the front of the sanctuary.

Each week, as the Sunday school hour ended, the classes would form an assembly in the sanctuary, and I would offer a brief report. And at the end, I would also invite those who were celebrating birthdays that week to come forward and place a dollar into a "blessing box"—which was, in actuality, a Mason jar.

These birthday celebrations were the highlight of the morning for me, but they also stood as a bright moment when I could witness individuals giving thanks for their lives and also receiving the cheers and good-natured jeers of others. The money collected in the blessing box was invariably given to assist with various mission work or community needs, and it was my duty to record these gifts also. Sometimes, the pastor referred to the blessing box in her sermon, and there were celebrations marked by what we had accomplished together.

The birth of Christ is the ultimate celebration. And in the birth of Jesus, we can mark the culmination of our life's greatest joys.

Blessings may be difficult to name, at times, but Christmas offers us special opportunities to become more acutely aware of God's gifts. And often, we become aware of these gifts as we realize how difficult life is and how much we are dependent upon the grace of God.

As we consider our struggles, challenges, and heartaches, and even the deeper pains of grief and loss, often our blessings bubble to the top. In a season of joy, despite the difficulties of the past, we sometimes are able to glimpse the wonderful blessings that flow into, and out of, our lives.

In fact, our lives are much like "blessing boxes"—receptacles of God's grace and beneficence. Our Creator deposits these blessings and offers them to us, without expectation of return or the promise of reciprocity.

On your journey to Bethlehem, pause for a moment to count your blessings and offer prayers of gratitude. Recounting God's wonderful gifts is truly what Christmas is all about.

Prayer

Praise God, from whom all blessings flow;
Praise God, all creatures here below;
Praise God above, all heavenly host;
Praise Father, Son, and Holy Ghost. Amen.

—The Common Doxology, adapted

Struggles

Then Joseph got up, took the child and his mother by night, and went to Egypt, and remained there until the death of Herod. This was to fulfill what had been spoken by the Lord through the prophet, "Out of Egypt I have called my son."

—MATTHEW 2:14-15

Some months ago, my adult son decided to enlist in the United States Marine Corps. This was a momentous decision for him, one fraught with internal conflict and anxiety. After enlisting, he had to leave behind the sunny beaches of Hawaii for a new life filled with mental and physical hurdles. In essence, he was leaving behind one way of life to embrace another. It was not easy.

We often forget that the journey to Bethlehem—or the journey to any destination or goal—is rarely a straight line. There can be deep valleys, enormous mountains to climb, pitfalls and detours.

It was this way for the Holy Family, as Matthew records that Mary and Joseph were forced to flee to Egypt with the infant Jesus. Before they could return to Galilee, they had to wait, watch, and listen. They had to discern, with God's guidance, what the proper time and timing would be.

This pattern that was true for Jesus is often present in our human experience as well. More than we care to admit, our faith rarely plays out in a straight and faithful line that sees us standing in good stead, full of confidence, hope, and joy. Rather, our experiences encompass lost opportunities, doubts, and sometimes extended periods of waiting. We are often uncertain of ourselves, of our decisions. We can often lack confidence in God.

The beginning for Jesus was filled with fear, darkness, and trepidation. Why should our experiences in life be any different? We frequently find that life does not give us what we had hoped for. We soon come to the realization that life is unfair, if not completely unpredictable and filled with anguish.

And still . . . we hope, even as Mary and Joseph held out hope. And hope is, perhaps, the greatest of God's gifts.

If we think about our struggles, we will soon realize that nothing worth having or obtaining is ever realized without them. Hardships produce character. And character, as the apostle Paul writes in Romans 5:1-5, produces hope.

Struggles? We are never without them.

But God gives us hope. And this hope will not disappoint us.

Prayer: *O Lord, take my struggles, my disappointments, and my days, and receive them as an offering of faith and confidence in your amazing grace. Help me realize that I do not have to be perfect in my ways to embrace your Way. I continue to walk the way of Bethlehem, with all of its detours and hardships, as I know I will find you, at last, at the end of my journey. In your name, I pray. Amen.*

Test

Therefore he had to become like his brothers and sisters in every respect, so that he might be a merciful and faithful high priest in the service of God, to make a sacrifice of atonement for the sins of the people. Because he himself was tested by what he suffered, he is able to help those who are being tested.

—HEBREWS 2:17-18

I don't know about you, but as a student, I always dreaded tests. There was a type of anxiety, a nervousness that would stymie my creativity and memory at the very thought of an upcoming test.

That is what makes this passage from Hebrews so remarkable. The thought that Jesus had to enter this world, into our humanity, our limitations, and our brokenness, and pass the test before God . . . this is remarkable. It is, perhaps, the most remarkable affirmation of Christmas. It is why we sing "Away in a Manger" or "Joy to the World" or "Silent Night." Christ entered the world; but he entered it as we all do—in the form of a helpless infant, fraught with the hungers and struggles and limitations that define our human predicament.

The gospel—in a nutshell—is here.

Jesus came to make atonement—to make us "at one with" God. This was not an easy test. It was not a rote assignment. There would be many hours and days of anguish. Jesus would have to walk with the same hungers, the same temptations, the same limitations as we encounter them.

And he passed the test.

How remarkable is this?

The writer of Hebrews does not downplay the suffering of Jesus but lifts his struggles all the higher, so we know that Jesus was not simply role-playing or serving as a character actor in some divine comedy. Christ's anguish was felt deeply, and still he embraced the test and passed through successfully.

In essence, Jesus gave everything he had. Even his very life.

This is the hallmark of Christmas. It is why we sing to Jesus and lift him up as the center of our worship and praise. He has shown us a path of humanity that is restored, forgiven, reconciled, and full of purpose.

Prayer: *Dear Jesus, thank you for passing the test on my behalf. I do not understand these mysteries, but I thank you for such amazing grace. Please use me—in spite of my sins, my brokenness, my limitations—to bring glory to you through my service and gratitude. Thank you for allowing me to walk this journey with you. Amen.*

Vision

Then I saw a new heaven and a new earth; for the first heaven and the first earth had passed away, and the sea was no more. And I saw the holy city, the new Jerusalem, coming down out of heaven from God, prepared as a bride adorned for her husband. And I heard a loud voice from the throne saying,

> *"See, the home of God is among mortals.*
> *He will dwell with them;*
> *they will be his peoples,*
> *and God himself will be with them;*
> *he will wipe every tear from their eyes.*
> *Death will be no more;*
> *mourning and crying and pain will be no more,*
> *for the first things have passed away."*

—REVELATION 21:1-4

Over the years, I have known many people who have sat vigil with loved ones who were dying. There has been grief, yes, but also hope . . . and sometimes vision.

We don't often equate the joys of Christmas with the promise of eternal joys in God's presence; but this vision, in part, is certainly connected to the songs we sing, the gifts we give and receive, and the delightful fruits of friendship. The promise of God's new creation comes full circle through the coming of Christ and the blessings of his fellowship.

One of the reasons that Christians, very early on, began to lengthen the celebration of Christmas (twelve days!) was because this vision could not be contained within a single day. There needed to be more time for reflection, for the giving and receiving of these blessings and realizations, and for opening our lives to the possibilities inherent in re-creating our lives and improving the misfortunes of others.

Christmas is not a day but an experience that pervades our lives by faith.

We are never far from these truths.

And, as it was with the physical journey to Bethlehem that Mary and Joseph once endured, any journey to Christ takes time. We always need more than a day to ponder the eternal significance of God's comfort and care.

The new creation has already begun. It is stirring inside of us now. New possibilities are emerging at every turn, every day.

Without this vision of what God can do and will do, we often search for meaning. God is already making all things new.

Prayer: *O God, remold and remake me today, that I may reflect, more and more, the likeness of your Son, Jesus. Help me to embrace this vision of your constant care and presence with me. Assist me in my grief as well as my joy. Inspire me in my service to others, and give me a greater awareness of your new creation. Amen.*

EIGHTH DAY
of Christmas

Transformation

I will turn their mourning into joy,
I will comfort them, and give them gladness for sorrow.

—JEREMIAH 31:13

Christmas is a season of transformation. We see this in the outward displays of light and festivity. We see it in the decoration of our homes and the aura of excitement that is evident in children. But we also see it in the nuances of changed behavior, in the willingness of people to become more generous, more neighborly, more forgiving and helpful.

The prophet Jeremiah had an even grander vision of transformation when he spoke of our sorrows. He envisioned God's comfort—a presence that would be far more than just a blanket for grief.

Several years ago, when our congregation organized a mission trip to Puerto Rico, I came face to face with God's comfort. Our group had been working with children all week in a small orphanage that was, at best, a meager haven to the dozens of children who lived there. The small staff of the orphanage was not equipped for the enormous task of teaching and supporting these children, and it was apparent that many of the children had deep relational and psychological scars.

At the end of our week, when our group said good-bye to these children, our grief, as well as the children's grief, was palpable. There were many tears, and as we parted, our group realized that we would not see these children again. Our work had been completed, and all we could do was make way for the next volunteer team to come in behind us.

However, as we left the orphanage that afternoon, a still breeze was blowing through the trees. And as we drove away, we looked back at the orphanage from our van. Suddenly, a white dove appeared, hovering over the orphans who had gathered in the yard, and our spirits were lifted. It was as if God was telling us all—there is more to every life than hardship and grief. God was telling us that there would be sorrow transformed into joy, that these children would be okay. We were not their salvation, just their helpers. God would do the rest.

How marvelous to remember these promises during the Christmas season, to delight in the gentle spirit of God's peace, and to know that nothing separates us from the love of God in Christ.

Sorrow can be transformed into joy. And joy comes with the morning.

Prayer: *Dear God, give me a greater sense of your peace today. Restore joy to those places in my life where grief has overtaken me. Do not give me over to despair, but renew the hope that is within me. This I ask in Jesus' name. Amen.*

The Blessed Life

Blessed be the God and Father of our Lord Jesus Christ, who has blessed us in Christ with every spiritual blessing in the heavenly places, just as he chose us in Christ before the foundation of the world to be holy and blameless before him in love.

—EPHESIANS 1:3-4

My grandmother was an astounding woman who, for more than forty years, taught in a one-room schoolhouse while helping my grandfather operate a country store, as well as being a wife, a mother, a grandmother, and a friend to many. She was also a lay preacher, who, during her lifetime, preached hundreds of revivals and funerals. When she died, I inherited her many sermon outlines, and her notes and journals on the Bible are among my most cherished possessions.

Reading through my grandmother's writings, I have noted how often she considered broken things: the cracked or shattered pieces of artifacts and of life that could be mended by God's love. She wrote many times of blessings and the manner in which God brings joys—often through hardship and pain.

Christmas is a season in which we often become more deeply aware of the anguish and brokenness of our world—while at the same time enjoying those spiritual blessings associated with God's intervention and care. At times, this can be an odd juxtaposition, but Christmas is a reminder that God did enter into the fullness of our human predicament and our experiences. We can trust God because God can give us the blessed life.

During these days when our attention is wrested away from the cares of the world, we may yet enjoy some sweet spirit of thoughtfulness or delight. These joys can be small things or subtle reminders that each day brings new opportunities and blessings—not just for ourselves but for the whole world.

The season also affords us the opportunity to leave the old behind in anticipation of embracing the new—and this too is a blessing. Refreshment. Renewal. Hope.

In this new day, perhaps we can also revive some spiritual practice that has been neglected or bring to light some dormant gift that has remained in the dark but could be offered to others—gifts such as praying for others, meditating on scripture, giving to the poor, and visiting the sick and the imprisoned.

Such is the gift of Christmas.

Prayer: *O God, may the spirit of Christmas wash over me today, offering hope to my spirit and vision to my thoughts. I not only ask to be blessed but also pray that I might especially be a blessing to others. May the hope of the Christ child enliven my steps and carry me forward into this new day of promise. Inspire me. Strengthen me. And embolden me to press on, even through the broken places. In Jesus' name, I pray. Amen.*

What's the Good Word?

In the beginning was the Word, and the Word was with God, and the Word was God. He was in the beginning with God.

—John 1:1-2

In my first pastoral appointment, I served a small, rural congregation that had employed an aged custodian to unlock the church building on Sunday mornings. This fellow, a bit curmudgeonly and terse, would often meet me at the front doors when I arrived, and he always greeted me with the same question each Sunday morning: "What's the good word today, pastor?"

His question always set me back on my heels a bit, but it also served to remind me that people *did* come to church expecting a good word—a gospel word. I was astounded, every week, that people showed up to hear my sermon—a good word, a proclamation from the Bible that might enliven or challenge them. Some folks even noted as they left church: "Thanks for getting my week off to a good start."

The Gospel of John begins much like this—with high expectations and a lofty vision of a living Word . . . the vision that Jesus is the living expression of God. The fourth Gospel hearkens back to Genesis, to the very beginning, and it shares the grand idea that God spoke through Jesus Christ from the beginning of creation. What a thought!

These ideas came full circle in the church through the centuries, with some theologians and thinkers—especially in the Middle Ages—expressing the concept that God was most accurately described as hidden but revealed in Christ. They found these ideas in the Gospel of John, a Gospel that begins with the idea that God was revealed in the Word made flesh.

So, what's the good word for today?

Perhaps it all depends upon our need and the experiences and opportunities that present themselves to us along the way. A good word could be a kind word or a handshake. It could be a cup of coffee and supportive conversation shared with a friend or with someone who is hurting. It might be a word of advice given or received. It might be kindness to a stranger or encouragement to someone who is broken or depressed. It might be an invitation or a welcome home. It might even be a final farewell or a sympathetic tear.

There is much to be celebrated today! A word—especially the living Word—can make all the difference in the world.

Prayer: *God of wonders, I am eager to receive good news today, and I am equally eager to pass it along. Open my ears to hear; open my eyes to see. Let me be fully present—to you and with others. Bless me, that I might be a blessing to others. Amen.*

Presents or Presence

The Word became flesh and lived among us, and we have seen his glory, the glory as of a father's only son, full of grace and truth.

—JOHN 1:14

Christmas is a season of gift giving and gift receiving. Presents are often placed under the tree or upon the mantel, and there is a sense of love in the sharing.

It is no wonder that presents have found their way into our Christmas traditions. Our gifts serve to remind us that God gave the gift of Jesus—and, subsequently, others gave too: Mary, Joseph, the magi, and all who made their way to Bethlehem.

It is *presence*, the very presence of God (*Emmanuel*), that is the hallmark of this season.

Throughout the ages, many others have given too. There have been disciples, sages, and humble servants of every nation and tongue who have given themselves to Christ.

Saint Francis of Assisi (1181/1182–1226 CE) was one such giver, a young man who denied his family's wealth and station to pursue a life of humility and devotion to Christ. Francis had no following at first, no disciples, and so he made his congregation the beasts of the field and the birds of the air, preaching a simple message of service to all who would listen.

The poems and hymns attributed to Francis are wonderful reminders that we too can be present for, and with, others. We can walk in the footsteps of Jesus. We can cherish his work and try to emulate his example.

There is a beautiful prayer that has become a favorite of many. It is believed to have been written long after Saint Francis's time, yet it has somehow become closely associated with him, including through its name. This prayer serves to remind us that when we are present with God, God can also be present with others. We can become instruments—servants—whom God can use; and as such, God will be present in the world, once again, through our hands and feet.

Prayer

Lord, make me an instrument of your peace:
Where there is hatred, let me sow love;
Where there is injury, pardon;
Where there is discord, union;
Where there is doubt, faith;
Where there is despair, hope;
Where there is darkness, light;
Where there is sadness, joy.

O divine Master, grant that I may not so much seek
To be consoled as to console,
To be understood as to understand,
To be loved as to love.
For it is in giving that we receive,
It is in pardoning that we are pardoned,
And it is in dying that we are born to eternal life.
Amen.

—Prayer of Saint Francis

TWELFTH DAY
of Christmas

See the Light

Arise, shine; for your light has come,
and the glory of the LORD has risen upon you.

—ISAIAH 60:1

When I was a teenager, I enjoyed camping with my friends. Often, much to the chagrin of our parents, my friends and I would hike deep into the woods, leaving behind the trail and familiar territory. We loved the excitement and adventure of hiking through places we had never seen.

But once, we hiked so far into the woods that we lost our way. Worse yet, darkness descended upon us, and we were disoriented and frightened.

Fortunately, one of my friends—the oldest and wisest among us—was not shaken. He pointed out that the darkness might actually be helpful to us. "The darker it gets," he pointed out, "the more clearly we'll be able to see the stars and the lights of town."

Indeed, he was correct. The darkness did afford us the ability to see the glow of city lights and, high in the sky, the guiding orientation of Polaris, the North Star.

In the traditional Christmas song "The Twelve Days of Christmas," the singer's "true love" gives twelve drummers drumming on the final day. No doubt an allusion to the twelve apostles who proclaimed the good news of Jesus Christ, the song reminds us that our love and our light has come and that Jesus gives us many good gifts.

Indeed, there are many times in life when we feel frightened, lost, disoriented, confused, and, perhaps, unloved. But the glory of God has risen upon the darkened world like a guiding star, like an embracing and comforting light.

What a wonderful proclamation!

Consider the significance of this season in your life. Where has God led you? Where have you been? What dangers have been eluded? What light have you seen?

There may be many gifts you have received and others you have given. Much has happened. There is much to come.

Give thanks for the wonderful gift of God's guidance, the lordship and leadership of Jesus. He is still walking the way with you.

The Light has come.

Prayer: *Light of the world, shine upon me. Illumine my way as I make decisions and navigate this life as best I can by your grace. Let no darkness overtake me; but what I cannot ascertain, let your guiding light lead the way. Hear my prayer and my prayers for others whom I love. Amen.*

✴ THE EPIPHANY

Givers

In the time of King Herod, after Jesus was born in Bethlehem of Judea, wise men from the East came to Jerusalem, asking, "Where is the child who has been born king of the Jews? For we observed his star at its rising, and have come to pay him homage." . . .

When they saw that the star had stopped, they were overwhelmed with joy. On entering the house, they saw the child with Mary his mother; and they knelt down and paid him homage. Then, opening their treasure chests, they offered him gifts of gold, frankincense, and myrrh.

—MATTHEW 2:1-2, 10-11

While the Gospel of Matthew does not tell us much about the *magi*—these mysterious travelers from the East who came in search of the boy Jesus—there are a great many traditions and ideas—mostly in the form of art, drama, and song—that have endeared the drama of the Epiphany visitation. Epiphany, in the church calendar, falls in line after the twelve days of Christmas and serves as a brief season for Christians to explore the varied ways Jesus Christ was revealed to the nations as Savior of the world.

This is where the magi come in. Matthew tells us they came from the East (perhaps from the region of ancient Persia), following a star that guided them first to King Herod and, subsequently, to the biblical scholars who instructed them, more specifically, to go to a house. Here, the magi found Mary and the baby Jesus. We are told the magi came to pay homage, yes. And by tradition, these magi represented all of the human race, scattered across the world.

But they also came to give. This is apparent from the outset and also the result, as they opened their "treasure chests" and offered to the child their gold, frankincense, and myrrh.

To arrive from such a great distance with the express purpose to give—this is impressive. But we can miss the planned giving, the generosity, if we are too quick to judge the motive.

The magi came to give—and this is where this Epiphany story leaves us in its wake. What are our motives as we come to adore the Christ? Do we come to gawk or associate or simply to say that we have been in the presence of the famous? Or is there some sense of mystery and honor that comes from the journey itself—the journey to Bethlehem? Like the magi, have we come to give, to express some gratitude or thanksgiving that comes from a deep place of adoration and hope?

Before we close the book on another Advent and Christmas season; before we leave behind another year and run, headlong, into the new, perhaps we can pause to see how marvelous God's salvation is and how wondrous is the mystery of God's presence with us.

Prayer: *God of all creation, I have arrived at this juncture in my life having trusted you until now. Although I can bring little in comparison to the magnitude of your grace, I do bring myself, and I offer you the best that I have. Use me as a small light in the darkness, and help me to honor you each day as I follow Jesus through all the uncertainties and complications of this life. In Jesus' name, I pray. Amen.*

Questions
for Personal Reflection
and Small-Group Guide

F ollow this outline for six one-hour gatherings during the season
of Advent and Christmas. Group meetings can be led by a des-
ignated leader or rotated among members of the group each week.
Gather in a comfortable place and, if possible, have group members
form a circle. You may choose to light a candle at the beginning of
each session.

WEEK ONE

Opening (5 minutes)

Read the words of Luke 2:15 together: "Let us go now to Bethlehem and see this thing that has taken place, which the Lord has
made known to us." Pause for silent prayer, asking God to open
your minds and hearts and lead you to new moments of discovery.

Preparing (10 minutes)

As you have prepared for this week's challenges and needs with
your family, at work, or in your celebrations, what experiences have
shaped your expectations or made you aware of God's guidance?

Which devotion from this week's readings spoke to you in an especially noteworthy way, and in what ways did it do so?

Listening (20 minutes)

Use the following questions in a time of engagement with the group, focusing on hearing and understanding the insight of your fellow group members.

1. What does "Advent" mean to you?
2. What transforming experiences have you had in life?
3. Why do you think charity (love, giving) comes alive during this season?
4. What type of distractions and opportunities do you think people experience today?
5. What attitudes and experiences do you think make harmony elusive today?
6. What "signs of God's love" have marked your life so far?
7. In what ways is fear the antithesis of faith?

Growing (15 minutes)

Ask someone to read aloud Mark 1:1-8.

What experiences make the first week of Advent a challenge? What experiences make it meaningful?

Going (5 minutes)

Share prayer concerns among the group, and close your meeting with a prayer.

WEEK TWO

Opening (5 minutes)

Read the words of Luke 2:15 together: "Let us go now to Bethlehem and see this thing that has taken place, which the Lord has made known to us." Pause for silent prayer, asking God to open your minds and hearts and lead you to new moments of discovery.

Preparing (10 minutes)

As you have prepared for this week's challenges and needs with your family, at work, or in your celebrations, what experiences have shaped your expectations or made you aware of God's guidance? Which devotion from this week's readings spoke to you in an especially noteworthy way, and in what ways did it do so?

Listening (20 minutes)

Use the following questions in a time of engagement with the group, focusing on hearing and understanding the insight of your fellow group members.

1. What big decisions are weighing on your life right now? How is God guiding you?
2. What adversities has God helped you overcome?
3. How would you describe the values that have shaped your life?
4. Why do you think fear is so pervasive and powerful?
5. What preparations have you been making to proclaim faith in your family celebrations?

6. As you have experienced life, what are some high points and some low points you could share?
7. How have you experienced God's time (or timing) in your life and decisions and outcomes?

Growing (15 minutes)

Ask someone to read aloud Jeremiah 31:31-34.

What experiences have made the second week of Advent meaningful? challenging?

Where might God be leading you?

Going (5 minutes)

Share prayer concerns among the group, and close your meeting with a prayer.

WEEK THREE

Opening (5 minutes)

Read the words of Luke 2:15 together: "Let us go now to Bethlehem and see this thing that has taken place, which the Lord has made known to us." Pause for silent prayer, asking God to open your minds and hearts and lead you to new moments of discovery.

Preparing (10 minutes)

As you have prepared for this week's challenges and needs with your family, at work, or in your celebrations, what experiences have shaped your expectations or made you aware of God's guidance? Which devotion from this week's readings spoke to you in an especially noteworthy way, and in what ways did it do so?

Listening (20 minutes)

Use the following questions in a time of engagement with the group, focusing on hearing and understanding the insight of your fellow group members.

1. How has the Holy Spirit led you in your life and decisions?
2. How has gratitude made a difference in your life?
3. As you are comfortable sharing with others, tell how God has restored or renewed you.
4. In what ways does Jesus still capture your wonder and imagination?
5. What is the best greeting that you have ever received, and what made it so?
6. What do you appreciate—or what would you like to celebrate—about your family?
7. What dreams or expectations are you placing in God's hands?

Growing (15 minutes)

Ask someone to read aloud Luke 1:26-38.

How has this third week of Advent been challenging? meaningful? Where might God be leading you?

Going (5 minutes)

Share prayer concerns among the group, and close your meeting with a prayer.

WEEK FOUR

Opening (5 minutes)

Read the words of Luke 2:15 together: "Let us go now to Bethlehem and see this thing that has taken place, which the Lord has made known to us." Pause for silent prayer, asking God to open your minds and hearts and lead you to new moments of discovery.

Preparing (10 minutes)

As you have prepared for this week's challenges and needs with your family, at work, or in your celebrations, what experiences have shaped your expectations or made you aware of God's guidance? Which devotion from this week's readings spoke to you in an especially noteworthy way, and in what ways did it do so?

Listening (20 minutes)

Use the following questions in a time of engagement with the group, focusing on hearing and understanding the insight of your fellow group members.

1. How do you draw strength and insight from God's creation?
2. How does the approach of Christmas Day change your outlook and preparations toward Jesus?
3. How does Mary inspire you?

4. Where and how do you need more patience in your life?
5. Where are you finding hope in your family?
6. How would you describe the ways that God has saved you?
7. What traditions do you and your family observe on Christmas Eve? Why these particular traditions?

Growing (15 minutes)

Ask someone to read aloud Luke 1:39-50.

How has this Advent season been challenging? meaningful? Where might God be leading you?

Going (5 minutes)

Share prayer concerns among the group, and close your meeting with a prayer.

WEEK FIVE

Opening (5 minutes)

Read the words of Luke 2:15 together: "Let us go now to Bethlehem and see this thing that has taken place, which the Lord has made known to us." Pause for silent prayer, asking God to open your minds and hearts and lead you to new moments of discovery.

Preparing (10 minutes)

As you have prepared for this week's challenges and needs with your family, at work, or in your celebrations, what experiences have shaped your expectations or made you aware of God's guidance?

Which devotion from this week's readings spoke to you in an especially noteworthy way, and in what ways did it do so?

Listening (20 minutes)

Use the following questions in a time of engagement with the group, focusing on hearing and understanding the insight of your fellow group members.

1. In what ways (and how) is Jesus still capturing your heart and imagination?
2. How has God blessed your family through the generations?
3. How would you describe God's power?
4. What blessings are you most grateful for?
5. What challenges has God helped you to overcome?
6. How do you see Jesus in light of his humanity?
7. Where do you see God at work in the world today?

Growing (15 minutes)

Ask someone to read aloud Luke 2:1-20.

What has made this Christmas season challenging? What has made it meaningful? Where might God be leading you?

Going (5 minutes)

Share prayer concerns among the group, and close your meeting with a prayer.

WEEK SIX

Opening (5 minutes)

Read the words of Luke 2:15 together: "Let us go now to Bethlehem and see this thing that has taken place, which the Lord has made known to us." Pause for silent prayer, asking God to open your minds and hearts and lead you to new moments of discovery.

Preparing (10 minutes)

As you have prepared for this week's challenges and needs with your family, at work, or in your celebrations, what experiences have shaped your expectations or made you aware of God's guidance? Which devotion from this week's readings spoke to you in an especially noteworthy way, and in what ways did it do so?

Listening (20 minutes)

Use the following questions in a time of engagement with the group, focusing on hearing and understanding the insight of your fellow group members.

1. How has God turned certain sadness into other joys in your life?
2. How would you describe "the blessed life" to another person?
3. What is the best news you have heard or received this week?
4. In what ways has God been present with you in this past year?
5. What is your favorite Christmas carol/hymn, and why?

6. Where are you seeing the light of Christ at work in your family? Your church?
7. What does the idea of "Epiphany" mean to you?

Growing (15 minutes)

Ask someone to read aloud Matthew 1:18-25.

How have these last days of Christmas and the first days of the new year been challenging? How have they been meaningful? Where might God be leading you?

Going (5 minutes)

Share prayer concerns among the group, and close your meeting with a prayer.

ABOUT THE AUTHOR

Todd Outcalt is a United Methodist pastor, artist, and author of more than forty books in six languages. His many titles include *Blue Christmas, Praying Through Cancer, Common Ground, The Other Jesus, Candles in the Dark,* and *Before You Say "I Do."* He also writes children's biographies, including *All About Martin Luther King, Jr.* and *All About Mohandas Gandhi.* Among the many magazines he has written for are *The Christian Century, Preaching, Youth Minister, Group,* and *The Christian Science Monitor.* In addition, Todd has completed the three great pilgrimages of Christendom— to Jerusalem, Rome, and the Camino de Santiago. He lives in Brownsburg, Indiana, with his wife, Becky.

NOTES

1. Spencer Johnson, *Who Moved My Cheese?* (New York: G.P. Putnam's Sons, 1998), 48.
2. (UMH, no. 553)